Compiled by Julia Skinner

With particular reference to the work of Malcolm Neesam and Roly Smith

THE FRANCIS FRITH COLLECTION

www.francisfrith.com

Based on a book first published in the United Kingdom in 2004 by The Francis Frith Collection®

This edition published exclusively for Identity Books in 2010 ISBN 978-1-84589-518-1

British Library Cataloguing in Publication Data

Did You Know? Harrogate - A Miscellany
Compiled by Julia Skinner
With particular reference to the work of Malcolm Neesam and Roly Smith

The Francis Frith Collection
Frith's Barn, Teffont,
Salisbury, Wiltshire SP3 5QP
Tel: +44 (0) 1722 716 376
Email: info@francisfrith.co.uk
www.francisfrith.com

Printed and bound in Malaysia

Front Cover: **HARROGATE, ROYAL PUMP ROOM 1902** 48975p

The colour-tinting is for illustrative purposes only, and is not intended to be historically accurate

AS WITH ANY HISTORICAL DATABASE, THE FRANCIS FRITH ARCHIVE IS CONSTANTLY BEING CORRECTED AND IMPROVED, AND THE PUBLISHERS WOULD WELCOME INFORMATION ON OMISSIONS OR INACCURACIES

CONTENTS

INTRODUCTION

Harrogate is one of the oldest of the English spa towns. One factor seems to have made Harrogate stand apart from other fashionable spas of the Georgian era, such as Bath: there appears to have been a more democratic and less formal air about the process of taking the waters here. George Carey, describing his visit in 1796, wrote: 'There is little etiquette at Harrowgate, nor are the company pestered with the officious and interested cringings of an obsequious Master of Ceremonies'. At this time, most spas in Britain appointed a Master of Ceremonies, usually a man of high social standing, to 'educate' the visiting public in matters of polite behaviour and decorum. Harrogate refused to dictate to its visitors in that overbearing manner, and allowed each hotel to elect its own Master of Ceremonies from among its guests, usually resulting in the longest-staying guest gaining the post, whatever his standing in society. By the time Queen Victoria ascended to the throne in 1837, the population of Harrogate had risen to just over 4,000, yet it still retained that rural character which so endeared itself to visitors. Dr Granville, in a survey of British spas in 1841, noted: 'Harrogate has the elements of becoming a Spa of the first magnitude, even to the extent of attracting foreign travellers ... It is not one of your ephemeral Spas, dependent on fashion ... it remains a village. Those (the waters) of Harrogate are unsophisticated because the place itself remains as it was.'

After the Second World War, Harrogate Corporation was quick to realise that the golden days of the town as a spa for the rich and famous were well and truly over. In fact, the town undoubtedly benefited from the post-war introduction of the National Health Service, and it became the country's largest centre for research into rheumatic diseases when half of the Royal Bath Hospital was converted into a research clinic. The 'cure' which had attracted visitors to Harrogate for so many years had become the property of the nation, and by 1959, 80% of Harrogate's patients received their treatment on the NHS. But Harrogate's city fathers knew its future lay elsewhere, and began the long process of reinventing the town to suit the fast-changing modern world. The town's tourist advertising changed from its being described as 'The Queen of the Inland Spas' to 'Britain's Floral Resort', in recognition of its fine parks and gardens. The first Northern Antique Dealers Fair took place in 1950, and the annual event now attracts over 10,000 visitors every April. Harrogate had always been the home of high-class shopping, but with the opening in 1998 of the elegant Victoria Shopping Centre on the site of the old market in 1992 and the new Marks & Spencer store on the site of the Victorian Lowther Arcade in 1998, the town's reputation for 'retail therapy' was beginning to match its medicinal therapies of the past. Harrogate is also now one of Britain's premier conference and exhibition centres, attracting such prestigious events as the conferences of the major political parties, in addition to many international exhibitions and fairs. The cultural highlight of Harrogate's year is the Harrogate International Festival, which was initiated in 1966. The varied programme includes classical music, dance, jazz, theatre, comedy, literature and crime writing, with the Harrogate Fiesta in Valley Gardens providing something for all the family.

However, Harrogate still retains its air of Victorian and Edwardian gentility which harks back to the golden years when it was Britain's premier inland spa. Although 'taking the waters' is no longer the main reason why thousands visitors now come to the town, that genteel heritage is never far from the surface as they walk its streets and perhaps visit the Royal Pump Room Museum, the Mercer Art Gallery, or stroll through the Valley Gardens or on the Stray. Echoes of that past are still provided by the magnificent, recently restored Turkish baths in the Royal Baths Assembly Rooms – a £1 million refurbishment has brought them back to their colourful Victorian glory. Visitors can now once again 'detox' in the steam room, relax in the three hot rooms and finally take a dip in the plunge pool of Baggalley and Bristowe's 1897 arabesque masterpiece.

Harrogate's reputation as 'England's Floral Town' perhaps stems from the establishment of the Northern Horticultural Society's 68-acre trial gardens at Harlow Carr in 1949, where TV gardener Geoffrey Smith was once superintendent. Now run by the RHS, Harlow Carr includes a beautiful streamside garden, a woodland arboretum, ornamental gardens, and several national collections of plants. The first Harrogate Spring Flower Show was held in 1927, and takes place every April at the Great Yorkshire Showground. The beauty of the town's meticulously maintained flower beds and displays is well-known, and in 2003 Harrogate won the coveted Britain in Bloom gold medal. The best time to visit Harrogate is undoubtedly in the spring, when the 200-acre Stray bursts into glorious colour as millions of crocuses and daffodils planted by the council come into bloom – a sight unmatched in any other British town or city.

HARROGATE, PARLIAMENT STREET 1907 58649

YORKSHIRE WORDS AND PHRASES

'A brussen tup' - someone who is full of his own importance.

'Ah'm sad flayed' - I'm a bit stupid.

'Bahn' - to go somewhere.

'Baht' - without.

'Bairn' - a baby.

'Clemmed' - very cold, frozen through.

'Featherlegged'- very tired.

'Fuzzock' - a donkey.

'Gennel' or 'ginnel' - a narrow alley or passageway between houses.

'Gerrod o' thissen' - sort yourself out, get a grip.

'Get agate then' - get on with it.

'Ippens' - nappies.

'Laike' - play, 'Laikin' - skiving off school or work.

'Leit green' - crafty, cunning.

'Mardy' - peevish, querulous, miserable, moody, sulking.

'Moudiwarp' - a mole.

'Muckment' - rubbish, refuse.

'Nesh' - feeling the cold, as in 'I'm a bit nesh'.

'Put 't wood in 't 'oil!' - close the door!

'Sackless' - lazy.

'Shuck' - crazy'.

'Snicket' - a pathway, between hedges, fences etc.

'Tewit' - a lapwing, after the sound these birds make (as in the Tewit Well at Harrogate).

'Tyke' - the broad Yorkshire dialect.

HARROGATE, ROYAL HALL GARDENS 1925 78967

HAUNTED HARROGATE

A report by paranormal investigators commissioned in 2005 by the television channel Sky Travel to publicise its 'Mysterious Britain' season found that Yorkshire is the second most haunted place in Britain after Cornwall, and that reports of ghost sightings were most common in the area between York, Leeds and Harrogate. One of the most famous haunted locations in Harrogate itself is the Harrogate Theatre in Oxford Street, originally constructed in 1900 as the Royal Opera House. The building's resident ghost is said to be friendly, and is known by the theatre staff as 'Alice'. Who she was in her earthly life remains a mystery – perhaps she was an actress, an usherette or even the lady-friend of someone connected with the theatre, but it appears that she threw herself to her death from the theatre's balcony – or was she pushed...? Whether her death was suicide or murder is not known either, but her unquiet spirit is said to manifest itself as a smell which can be detected in a corridor in the theatre.

Another famous haunted location in the Harrogate area is the now-ruined fortified manor house known as Spofforth Castle, 3½ miles south-east of Harrogate, off the A661, which was once the home of the Percy family. The ruins are said to be haunted by a greyish apparition in vaguely human shape, which has been seen standing on the parapet at the top of the tower before falling to the ground – perhaps a ghostly re-enactment of an act of suicide in the past. This phenomenon was witnessed in 1969 by a group of schoolchildren and their teacher, and again in 1973, when it startled two people enjoying a picnic there.

Ripley Castle, three miles north of Harrogate off the A61, is said to be haunted by a ghostly lady in Victorian dress who walks across the hallway; she is believed to be the restless shade of Lady Alicia Ingilby, who lived at the castle in the 1870s, and whose two children tragically died there. She is said to be a benevolent spirit, who wanders the castle keeping a ghostly eye on the welfare of present-day children living there.

HARROGATE, STATION SQUARE 1921 71649

George Dalton
TETLEY & SONS
CIGARS & TOBACCOS

HARROGATE, JAMES STREET 1914 67283

HARROGATE, PARLIAMENT STREET
1923 74570

HARROGATE MISCELLANY

The earliest evidence of human settlement that has yet been found in the area is the so-called Harrogate Hoard of spearheads dating from the Bronze Age, uncovered at Bilton in 1848.

Bilton, to the north of the present town of Harrogate, had an Anglo-Saxon foundation. The name means 'Billa's enclosure', and the first mention of what is now Harrogate occurs when Bilton is referred to in a document of AD972, which details the territories of church lands belonging to Northumbria.

The River Nidd has an ancient Celtic name which is thought to mean 'brilliant water', or what we might today call 'sparkling'.

What is now Harrogate formed the central part of the royal hunting Forest of Knaresborough, governed from the stronghold of Knaresborough Castle, built on its hill above the River Nidd during the 12th century.

The Domesday Book contains references to land-holdings in what was later to become Harrogate, recording the two hamlets of Bilton and Beckwith-with-Rossett, including Pannal.

Haverah Park, included within the Royal Forest boundary, was granted by Henry II to William de Stuteville in 1173. Fodder from Haverah Park was reserved for horses in the royal stud, according to records from 1318-19 during the reign of Edward II.

One interpretation of the name Harrogate (there are several theories) is that it might mean 'the road to Haverah', where the so-called John of Gaunt's Castle was probably only a hunting lodge, almost certainly used by Edward II when he was recorded as travelling along the 'Harlow Gatte' from Knaresborough in 1323.

The first written historical reference to a place named 'Harrogate' occurs for September 1322, when 'John of Harrogate' was arraigned before the Forest Court in a case of assault and trespass.

In the Middle Ages coal and timber from Harrogate Park helped to power the local forging industry in Nidderdale, and coal was still being taken from Bilton Park as late as the end of the 18th century.

The Black Death, which reached Yorkshire in 1349, hit the Harrogate area hard. No figures have survived of the death rate, but some indication of its effect can be seen in the Court Rolls of 1349-50, which record that of the 575 acres which made up Bilton-with-Harrogate, 274 acres were held by tenants who had died in the horrendous outbreak.

HARROGATE, HARLOW MANOR HYDRO
1902 48986

HARROGATE, VICTORIA BATHS 1888 20940

'Assarting' is the medieval name for the winning of new farmland from the waste or forest. Where it took place can often be recognised in surviving place names, such as 'stocks', 'stubs' and 'stubbing' – which refer to the stumps of felled trees, particularly in the north of England. Local examples include Rudding Park, Hapsthwaite and Brackenthwaite, 'thwaite' deriving from an Old Norse name for a forest clearing.

A survey of the park at Bilton in 1476 found that it was 'gretely hurted and the woods therof almost destroid by felling of the grete trees' and that the pasture of the same park 'is gretely hurted by wroting of swine.'

Poaching of the king's forest deer was a problem in medieval times. In a case heard in 1482 several men were accused, including the Minister of St Robert's Church at Pannal, of the hunting and killing of deer at Harlow and Haverah.

Farming was still the most common source of employment and income for the people of the scattered communities which made up present-day Harrogate during the 15th century. Other activities included forestry, weaving and the forging of iron, although the use of timber as a fuel source seems to have died out by the late 14th century. It was replaced by coal and peat extracted from the forest at places like Bilton. Ironstone was also found within the forest boundaries. The name of nearby Kirkby Overblow, a village to the south of Harrogate, means 'the village with a church and smelters'. Prospecting for ironstone within the forest attracted the attention of the Duchy of Lancaster as a potentially lucrative source of income. It was later said that 'many iron-stones were thrown up' and that 'all the ground thereabout being formerly digg'd up, and all the wood destroyed in Queen Elizabeth's time, by iron-forges'. The Duchy appointed a surveyor, Richard Stanhope, to look into the situation in the Harrogate area in the later 16th century, and it may well have been the search for ironstone which inadvertently was the cause of the discovery of Harrogate's earliest mineral springs. Of course, we cannot know four centuries on exactly how William Slingsby of Bilton Park came across the first chalybeate (iron-rich water) spring in the area still known as Bilton-with-Harrogate in 1571, but we do know that the prospecting for ironstone was very intense in the forest at the time. Maybe he was attracted by the flocks of lapwings (known locally as 'tewits' in imitation of their call) which periodically gathered around the spring to taste the salty crystals which formed from the chalybeate water around its edges. And perhaps it was for that reason that he named the spring the Tewit Well.

Dr Edmund Deane of York's 1626 'Spadacrene Anglica – or The English Spaw Fountaine' was the first book to describe the medical benefits of the spa waters of the Harrogate area. Deane refers to Slingsby's discovery of 55 years before 'at Haregatehead', and to its promotion by Dr Timothy Bright, the personal physician to 'Good Queen Bess', Queen Elizabeth I.

The word 'spa' comes from the Walloon (Belgium) 'espa' meaning a 'a fountain'. It was Dr Bright, the personal physician to Queen Elizabeth I, who was the first to refer to the Harrogate (or Knaresborough) wells as 'the English Spaw', which according to Malcolm Neesam was the first recorded application of the name to an English resort. Dr Bright became a keen drinker of the water himself.

The sulphurous waters from the Harrogate wells were a recommended cure for worms and other kinds of internal parasites, which in the late 17th century were said to have affected at least 80% of the population.

The Harrogate waters were not to the taste of the eminent botanist and naturalist John Ray, who recorded after his visit in 1661: ' …we visited the sulphur well, whose water, though it be pellucid enough, yet stinks noisomely like rotten eggs or sulphur auratum diaphoreticum.'

HARROGATE, ST PETER'S CHURCH 1927 80225

HARROGATE, CHILDREN'S POOL 1925 78971

Another visitor who was not impressed with the facilities of the spa was Lady Verney, who in 1665 reported:
'...the house and all that is in it being horridly nasty and crowded up with all sorte of company, which we Eate within a room as the spiders are redy to drop into my mouthe, and sure hathe nethor been well cleaned nor ared this doseuen yeres, it makes me moare sicke than the nasty water...'

People came to the spa not only to drink the water for health reasons but also to bathe in them to cure all kinds of skin complaints.

Harrogate claims to have the world's strongest known sulphur spring.

The present octagonal, domed building of the Royal Pump Room in Crown Place was designed in the classical style by Isaac Thomas Shutt, son of the licencee of the Swan Inn who discovered the controversial Thackway Well in 1835. It took the place of an old stone temple dating from 1808, which was removed and re-erected over the Tewit Well.

In 1660 the town constable claimed 7d (3p) for 'carrying one cripple to Harrogait on horseback'.

The Queen's Head on the road between Harrogate and Knaresborough became the first hotel to open in the late 17th century.

One of the most popular theories in the 18th century to explain Harrogate's famous mineral springs was that they were the result of timbers sunk deep underground, gradually rotting away beneath a bed of earth and moss. This was long before more scientific explanations proved that they were the result of magmatic or plutonic waters rising from deep within the earth's crust.

HARROGATE, ROYAL BATH HOSPITAL 1892 30627

HARROGATE, THE STRAY 1902 48967

Many famous people travelled to Harrogate to take the waters in its Georgian hey-day. Among them were General Robert Clive ('of India'), who stayed at the Granby in 1763; the novelist Tobias Smollett in 1766 (who later described his experiences in his novel 'Humphry Clinker'), and the poet Lord Byron, who stayed at the Crown in 1806.

Thomas Chippendale of Otley, the famous English cabinet-maker, designed the Tuscan-columned domed Roman temple which first enclosed the Old Sulphur Well in Low Harrogate in 1808. The building, on the site of the Royal Pump Room, was paid for by public subscription and completed in 1808.

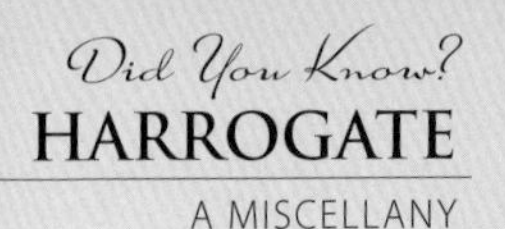

The first theatre was built in Harrogate as early as 1788, replacing the barn which has been utilised for that purpose at the front of the Granby Hotel in High Harrogate. It remains one of Harrogate's finest Georgian buildings, now a private dwelling known as Mansfield House.

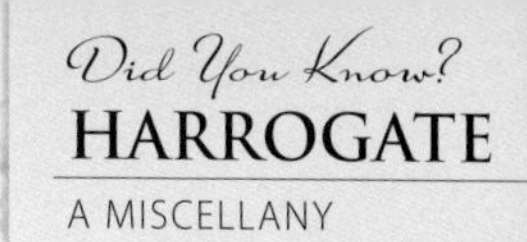

A racecourse was constructed on The Stray in 1793.

HARROGATE, STATION SQUARE 1902 48978

HARRROGATE, THE ROYAL PUMP ROOM 1923 74569

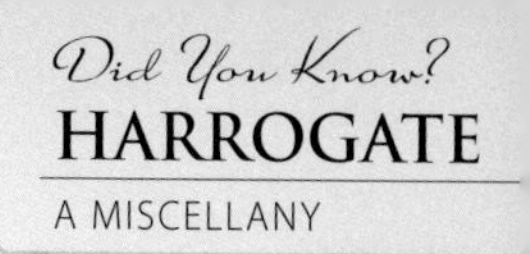

On of the great characters of 18th-century Harrogate was Jack Metcalf, better known as Blind Jack of Knaresborough, the famous sightless road-maker who was responsible for many of the turnpike roads constructed in the district, including the Boroughbridge turnpike and the road between Harrogate and Harewood Bridge. Jack hailed from nearby Knaresborough and had been blinded by smallpox at the age of six. He served as an engineer and bandsman under General Wade in Scotland, where he learnt the skills of road-building, and constructed about 200 miles/320km of roads in the north of England. He was invited to Harrogate to become the resident fiddler at the Queen's Head Hotel in 1732 and became a popular local celebrity at local inns and hotels. A big man (he weighed 17 stone) of many talents, he arranged the town's first transport hire service, and later scandalously eloped with the daughter of the Granby Hotel's landlord on the eve of her wedding.

Vandalism is not just a modern problem. In 1821-22 the townspeople of Harrogate complained to the Duchy of Lancaster that ' during the night time, some persons unknown to your petitioners have put into the said Mineral Springs, quantities of Dung, Ashes, Dead Dogs and other animals of a most offensive nature.'

In 1818 a committee was set up with the intention of opening a new subscription for the erection of baths which would be solely for the use of the poor. The new Bath Hospital, eventually to become the Royal Bath Hospital in Valley Gardens, opened for its for its first patients in 1826 – with a strict set of rules barring its patients from loitering around the wells and parks frequented by visitors.

In 1831 the dilapidated chapel of St John, which had been built on 1749 on Duchy of Lancaster land, was replaced by the Early English-style Christ Church in a triangular island on The Stray. The stone from the older building was re-used by the Congregationist church to build their new Providence chapel on the corner of John Street and James Street.

The tower of St Peter's Church, which dominates Prospect Place, was not added to the Victorian church until the 1920s.

In 1834, when the foundations of Joseph Thackwray's Tuscan-style Montpellier Baths were being dug, no fewer than six new wells were discovered, including four valuable new sulphur wells.

The rivalry between the two Harrogate entrepreneurs John Williams and Joseph Thackwray came to a head in 1835 when, shortly after the opening of William's Spa Rooms, it was discovered that the Old Sulphur Well was draining away. When the situation was investigated, it was found that Joseph Thackwray had ordered the digging of a well in a nearby shop, apparently to divert the waters from the public sulphur well onto his private estate. Thackwray was served with a notice to stop the work or face prosecution, and eventually the case of the 'Thackwray well' was heard at York Assizes in March 1827.

HARROGATE, PARLIAMENT STREET 1907 58649

HARROGATE, VIEW FROM PROSPECT HOTEL 1902 48970

The statue of Queen Victoria in Station Square was erected to mark the Queen's Golden Jubilee in 1887. Harrogate celebrated the occasion with an ox-roasting for the people of the town held on The Stray, provided by the benefactor Samson Fox. The spit holding the great carcass turned all day, as a band played to entertain the people, and free bread and beer was laid on. Fox also arranged displays of the new electric lighting to illuminate the scene.

One of the strangest things about Harrogate's famous mineral wells is that, of the scores of springs which reach the surface, no two are exactly identical in their chemical analysis.

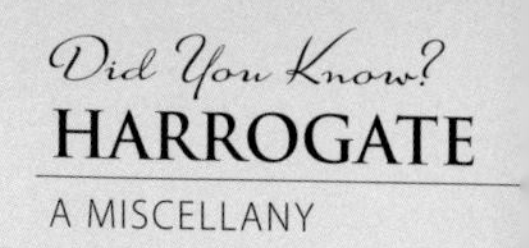

One of Harrogate's Victorian characters was Betty Lupton, the so-called 'Queen of the Well', who administered the waters with her long-handled spoon and cup for 56 years. When she retired in 1843 she was uniquely given a pension by the Commissioners.

Before the coming of the railway to Harrogate in 1848, visitors arrived by stage-coach, and the town's four coaching inns could accommodate up to 30 carriages with stabling for 100 horses. In 1838 there were 18 daily departures by stage coaches named 'Rocket', 'Dart', 'True Briton', 'Tally-ho' and 'Teazle' from Harrogate, to places as far away as Newcastle and Manchester, York, Leeds and Selby.

HARROGATE, CRESCENT GARDENS 1911 63514

There was considerable opposition among innkeepers and hoteliers to the coming of the railway to Harrogate. They feared the town would be flooded with a lower class of visitor from the new industrial towns of Leeds and Bradford. They also feared that the engines would frighten the grazing cattle on The Stray, and that the inferior incomers would bring their own food with them – and eat it in public.

The foundation stone for the new Royal Baths was laid on July 10th 1894. The building was fitted out in the greatest luxury, with polished marble pillars and floors, ornate plasterwork with classical inscriptions, and palm plants in abundance. Among the weird and wonderful treatments available to visitors in the opulent building were Aix-douche massages, Schnee baths, Greville baths, external douches, intestinal lavage, cataphoresis, and the dangerous-sounding static shocks and inhalation of radioactive gases.

By the end of the 19th century Harrogate had really begun to establish itself, especially among the rich and famous, and it was said that so many eminent statesmen were among its visitors that Queen Victoria could have held a Cabinet meeting there if she had wished. As it was, the Queen never actually visited Harrogate herself at any time during her 64-year reign.

The Royal Hall was originally called the Kursaal, or 'Cure Hall', a then fashionable German name for a spa assembly building. It was renamed the Royal Hall at the height of the anti-German feeling during the First World War, but the name 'Kursaal' remains in the stonework above the entrance.

HARROGATE, ROYAL PUMP ROOM
1914 67285

HARROGATE, CHILDRENS POOL, VALLEY GARDENS 1925 78970

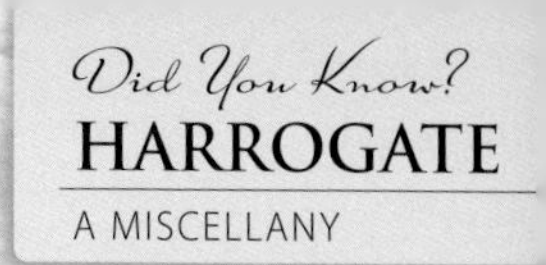

Entertainment in the Valley Gardens in the early 20th century included performances by Tom Coleman's Harrogate Pierrots seen in photograph 58645 below. The Pierrots dressed in clown suits of white with white conical hats, and wore the traditional clown's all-white face make-up. They played banjos and a hurdy-gurdy and sang the popular tunes of the day.

Sir Edward Elgar became a frequent visitor to Harrogate, although he noted rather sniffily that 'Harrogate thinks itself very fashionable and more than a little chic, and the ladies dress up terribly.' His Second Symphony was given its first provincial performance by the Harrogate Municipal Orchestra in 1911, conducted by Julian Clifford.

HARROGATE, VALLEY GARDENS 1907 58645

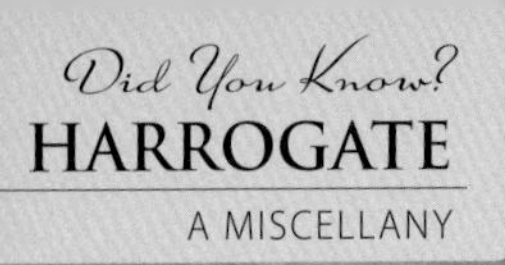

Harrogate attracted many royal visitors in the early 20th century, including Queen Alexandra, Empress Marie of Russia, Queen Amelie and King Manuel of Portugal, Princess Victoria, Prince Henry of Russia, and Prince Christopher of Greece.

In the early 20th century the building that dominated the town was the 400-bed Hotel Majestic, (fondly known as simply Number One, Harrogate, or less reverently as 'the Magic Stick'). The massive six-storeyed, copper-domed building opened its doors in July 1900. It cost the developer Sir Blundell Maple a staggering £250,000, but it really was the last word in luxury. At its centre was the 8,000sq ft Winter Garden, heralded as the largest glazed space in Yorkshire.

HARROGATE, ST PETER'S CHURCH 1927 80223

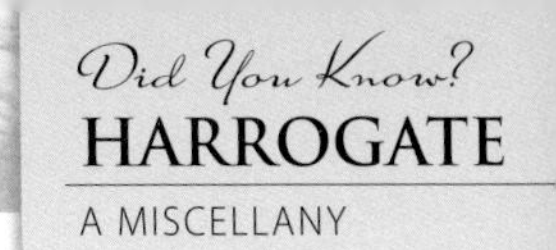

HARROGATE, PROSPECT PARK c1950 H26097

With the opening of the Kursaal (see page 32), Harrogate became something of a cultural centre for the north and such big names as Dame Nelly Melba, Sarah Bernhardt, Clara Butt, Lily Langtry and George Robey appeared on its stages.

During the First World War the 5th West Yorkshire Volunteers – also known as the Harrogate Pals – was formed almost entirely of young men from the town who went to fight, many never to return. The Centotaph in Prospect Place records over 800 names, the flower of Harrogate's youth.

HARROGATE, KURSAAL 1907 58657

HARROGATE, VALLEY GARDENS ENTRANCE 1928 81523

HARROGATE, PARLIAMENT STREET
c1955 H26125

SMITHS CELEBRATED TADCASTER ALES
Somerset
HOTEL
PEARL
ASSURANCE
COMPANY
Arthur English
AWP 428

SPORTING HARROGATE

The successful amateur level Harrogate District Swimming Club, based at the Hydro in Jennyfields Drive, was the first club in Yorkshire to achieve ASA Swim21 accreditation, the nationally recognised 'quality mark' showing that the club is committed to excellence in the areas of teaching, skill development, competitive development and performance. The club is producing a number of successful young swimmers, but a particular name to watch for the future is Lucy Budimir.

Harrogate's two football teams are Harrogate Town FC and Harrogate Railway Athletic FC. Harrogate Town (playing at Wetherby Road) was founded in 1914 as Harrogate AFC but this was disbanded in 1932. A football club was refounded in 1935 as Harrogate Hotspurs, and the name was changed to Harrogate Town FC in 1948. Harrogate Town FC is nicknamed 'The Sulphurites' after the sulphurous water that the town's spas were famous for. The club was knocked out of the FA Cup in the 2007-08 season by its local rival, Harrogate Railway Athletic FC, but has a respectable list of honours and has won the West Riding County Challenge Cup eight times to date. Harrogate Railway Athletic FC, nicknamed 'The Rail' or 'The Locomotives', was founded in 1935 as a workers team from Starbeck LNER locomotive shed, and in 1946 the side reached the British Railways National Cup Final. After this success the club planned to move to a new home elsewhere, but the LNER offered to lend the club the £1,500 needed to purchase its existing ground at Station View on condition that 300 rail workers contributed one penny from their wages each week towards the repayments. Enough volunteers agreed to this and the club still plays at its Station View ground. In the 2002-03 season Harrogate Railway reached the Second Round of the FA Cup before losing to Bristol City, and reached the Second Round again in the 2007-08 season before losing to Mansfield Town. Following promotion into the Northern Premier League First Division in 2005-06, Harrogate Railway played in the inaugural season of the Northern Premier League Division One North in 2007-08.

HARROGATE, ROYAL HOTEL 1924 75644

What is now Harrogate RUFC began life in 1871 as 'Harrogate Football Club' and played its first match in December of that year on the Stray. The Harrogate team for that first match included four brothers (from the Fawcett family), believed to be a club record that still stands. The rugby club moved to Claro Road in 1896 and an 'international' match between Harrogate and a team from Canada took place there in 1903, but sadly the result is not recorded. In 1906 the 2nd XV was formed into a team called Harrogate Old Boys, and after Harrogate Football Club turned to soccer in 1914, the rugby club continued playing under that name and purchased the Claro Road ground in 1926. In 1936 Harrogate Old Boys amalgamated with Harrogate RUFC, which was formed in 1923 and played at a ground at Knaresborough Road (now Shaw's caravan park). The rugby club's second team is known as the Georgians, in commemoration of a team of that name made up of ex-Civil Service personnel from St George's Road which joined with Harrogate RUFC in 1957. The club is particularly proud of its 'Bantams', the Mini/Junior section; when this was formed in the 1970s it was one of the first in the country, and it has produced some notable young players.

Although the earliest recorded reference to cricket being played in Harrogate was in 1846, the present Harrogate Cricket Club was not formed until 1877, with the Bilton Cricket Club being formed in the 1890s. Several England games were played at Harrogate CC's St George's Road ground between 1880 and 1902, and in 1885 the legendary W G Grace played there in the England team against Australia. The ground was also the venue for one Yorkshire County match each year until 1995. The club's website records that women first played cricket at the ground in 1890, with their long skirts weighed down with lead shot so that they did not flap about immodestly in the wind! A famous cricketer from the town was Maurice Leyland, born in New Park, Harrogate in 1900. He played in 41 Test matches for England between 1928 and 1938, was considered by many to have been one of the best left-handers of his generation, and was a Wisden Cricketer of the Year in 1929. During his career he made 33,660 runs in 686 first-class games, 26,191 of them being for Yorkshire County Cricket Club, but he was equally famous for his dry sense of humour. In the days before the wearing of protective helmets, he said of the courage needed to face the top-class fast bowlers: "Nobody likes 'em, but some of us don't let on."

QUIZ QUESTIONS

Answers on page 50.

1. The unusual structure of light brick on Montpellier Parade known as the Herald Building was once home to the Harrogate Herald newspaper, and still displays a sign on its façade advertising 'lists of visitors'. What did this mean?
2. What is the meaning of the Latin motto 'Arx Celebris Fontibus' in Harrogate's coat of arms?
3. Which famous novelist 'disappeared' in Harrogate in 1926?
4. The 200 acres of common land known as the Stray (meaning 'land grazed, or strayed over, by cattle') has been kept as a jealously guarded open space at the heart of Harrogate for use of the people of the town and its visitors for over 220 years. It is a facility which is the envy of many a larger city. It is probably only approached in its extent and usage by London's Royal Parks, but it is a fragile heritage on which constant vigilance has to be exercised. Why was the Stray Defence Association formed in 1932?
5. How was an unexploded German bomb removed from the Majestic Hotel in September 1940, during the Second World War?
6. What is Harrogate's connection with the long-running BBC radio serial, 'The Archers'?
7. Who are the figures depicted in the statue in Crescent Gardens (formerly known as Royal Hall Gardens) seen in photograph 78966 (right)?
8. According to his tombstone in Christ Church, William Hill, who died in 1868, was the 'Stray herdsman' for around 40 years. What did his job entail?
9. Harrogate is twinned with three other towns in the world – can you name them?
10. Who founded Harrogate's famous Bettys Tea Rooms?

HARROGATE, ROYAL HALL GARDENS 1925 78966

RECIPE

SUMMER PUDDING

Summer Pudding was a popular dessert with visitors to hydropathic establishments in spa towns such as Harrogate because it was lighter than pastry-based puddings, which were thought to be heavy and indigestible. For this reason it was sometimes known as Hydropathic Pudding.

10 slices of crustless white bread – use bread from a proper loaf, not a sliced and wrapped one, for best results

3 tablespoonfuls of milk

750g/1½ lbs soft fruit – use a variety of fruits such as raspberries, cherries, redcurrants, blackcurrants, white currants, loganberries or (sparingly) strawberries

115g/4oz caster sugar

Reserve a few pieces of fresh fruit to decorate.

Lightly butter a pudding basin of 1 litre (1¾ pint) capacity. Moisten the bread with milk. Hull, stone or top and tail the fruit as necessary. Cook it all very gently in a saucepan in the sugar for 4-5 minutes until the sugar melts and the juices run. Spoon off a few spoonfuls of the juice as it cools and reserve. Line the sides and bottom of the pudding basin with the bread slices, cutting them to fit where necessary and checking that there are no spaces. Reserve enough bread slices for a lid. Pour in the fruit, which should come almost to the top, and cover closely with the remaining bread. Put a small plate over the top (it should just fit inside the rim of the basin), and weight it with something heavy. Leave to press overnight in the fridge.

To serve, remove the weight and the plate. Place a deep serving dish over the top of the pudding basin and reverse quickly so that the pudding comes out easily in one piece. Pour the remaining juices slowly all over the pudding, especially over the places where the juice has not seeped through the bread slices thoroughly. Keep cold until ready to serve, then decorate with a few pieces of fruit and serve with cream.

RECIPE

WEST RIDING PUDDING

Harrogate was formerly in the old West Riding area of Yorkshire, which originally extended down to Sheffield. It was the Viking Danes who settled in Yorkshire in the Dark Ages who first divided the huge county into the three Ridings, or 'thridings' (thirds), and they became the North, East and West Ridings before these administrative areas were abolished under the local government reorganisation of 1974.

175g/6oz shortcrust pastry

2 tablespoonfuls of raspberry jam

115g/4oz butter

115g/4oz caster sugar

2 eggs, beaten

115g/4oz self-raising flour

25g/1oz ground almonds

Grated zest of half a lemon

Pre-heat the oven to 180°C/350°F/Gas Mark 4.

Roll out the pastry on a lightly floured surface, and use it to line a greased 20cm (8 inch) pie tin. Spread the base of the tart with raspberry jam.

Cream the butter and sugar together in a bowl until the mixture is light and fluffy. Beat in the eggs a little at a time, adding a little flour if necessary to prevent curdling. Sift the flour into the mixture, then add the ground almonds and grated lemon zest, and gently fold it all in. Turn the mixture into the pie tin and spread it over the jam. Bake in the pre-heated oven for 25-30 minutes, until the filling is well risen and firm and the pastry is golden and crisp.

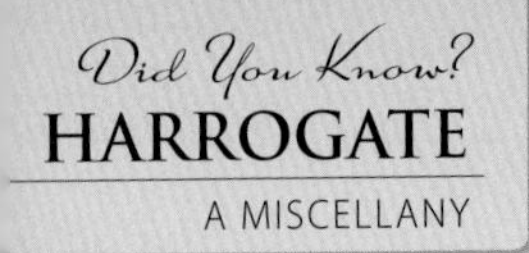

QUIZ ANSWERS

1. The 'list of visitors' sign on the façade of the Herald Building refers to the lists that used to be published by the Harrogate Herald which contained details of the names and origins of all visitors to the spa resort of Harrogate, together with the names of the hotels where they were staying. These lists enabled visitors to scan the names of visitors at other hotels, and if they knew them, to send an invitation to attend their hotel's ball night, which the invited guest would then reciprocate, as all the big Harrogate hotels formerly used to provide ball nights. In this way, visitors were able to attend the entertainments of several evenings.

2. 'The city (or centre) famous for its springs'. The town's coat of arms was adopted when Harrogate became incorporated as a borough in 1884, and also features two wells and two hunting horns, recalling the importance of the spa wells to the town and also its ancient origins as part of the Royal Forest of Knaresborough.

3. Agatha Christie. The popular crime novelist's most famous mystery story concerned herself, and a secret trip to Harrogate in 1926. Agatha Christie went missing from her London home for 10 days, apparently troubled by the death of her mother, overwork, and troubles in her marriage to Colonel Christie. Allegedly, she saw a poster advertising Harrogate on Waterloo Station and resolved on the spot to go there. She stayed at the Swan Hydro, now the Old Swan Hotel, assuming the name of her husband's mistress, Theresa Neele. Apparently she enjoyed the varied social life that the spa could offer a young woman at the time. Eventually she was recognised and returned to her husband, whom she divorced two years later. The story was filmed as 'Agatha' in 1977, starring Vanessa Redgrave and Dustin Hoffman.

4. After the council had dug up part of the Stray for flowerbeds. According to the respected local historian Malcolm Neesam, 'The Battle of The Stray' has to be fought about once every decade as it falls victim to the whims and fancies of whatever new pet scheme a new coterie of councillors may come up with. In his 1989 book 'Exclusively Harrogate', he urges local people to resist any attempts by the council to encroach upon the Stray: "As in the past, so for ever should the public answer be 'not a blade of grass, not an inch of soil - the Stray is not negotiable'."

5. During the Second World War, an unexploded bomb which landed on the Hotel Majestic on 12 September 1940 was found standing upright in an upstairs room of the hotel by soldiers sent to investigate. At first, Captain G H Yates and Eric Stirk mistook it for a water tank, and they used the hotel lift to take it out! After the bomb had been safely defused, the casing was used to raise money for the Harrogate Spitfire Fund. Captured German documents revealed that the Germans had believed that the hotel was being used by the Air Ministry, but a newspaper claimed at the time that the pilot of the bomber had once been refused a table at the Majestic's restaurant when he had called before the war, and had targeted the hotel in revenge.

6. The signature tune of 'The Archers' was composed by Arthur Wood, a former choirboy at St Peter's Church, sometime solo pianist in the Valley Gardens, and later deputy conductor of the Harrogate Municipal Orchestra, who became a well-known composer. Among his best-known works was 'My Native Heath', which was about his homeland of Yorkshire. The movement entitled 'Barwick Green' was originally written as a tune for a maypole dance, but became better known as the signature tune for what is now the longest-running radio series in the world, 'The Archers'.

7. This white marble statue by the Italian master Giovanni Maria Benzoni in the Crescent Gardens (formerly known as the Royal Hall Gardens) in the centre of town shows Cupid and Psyche, figures from Roman mythology. The statue is now sheltered from the elements by an ornate modern cupola, but when this photograph was taken in 1925 it still stood unprotected in a flowerbed. Psyche was a young woman so beautiful that she incurred the jealous wrath of the goddess Venus, who sent her son Cupid to make Psyche fall in love with a loathsome creature. Her plan went astray when Cupid himself fell in love with Psyche and could not carry out his mother's command. After many trials and tribulations the couple were eventually given permission to marry by Jupiter, king of the Roman gods, and lived happily ever after.

8. The 200-acre Stray in Harrogate was opened for public use in 1778, but a number of local families retained grazing rights, known as 'gates'. There were fifty gates, each entitling the owner to graze either one cow, or a two-year-old horse, or four sheep. Gates were property, and as such could be bought or sold or rented out. All the animals on the Stray were looked after by a herdsman, such as William Hill. The Stray herdman's job would have been to attend to all the animals legitimately placed on the Stray by the gate holders. His duty was to exclude donkeys, mules, pigs, goats and geese, and he was empowered to impound any animal grazing on the Stray illegally – or 'gate-crashing', as it was known.

9. Harrogate is twinned with Luchon in France, Wellington in New Zealand and Harrogate, Tennessee in the United States of America.

HARROGATE, PROSPECT HOTEL 1891 28309

10. No one knows for sure who the 'Betty' of Harrogate's world-famous Bettys Tea Rooms was. The business began in 1919 when Frederick Belmont, a Swiss confectioner who married his landlady's daughter when he came to Yorkshire in 1907, set up his first Continental-style tearooms in Cambridge Crescent, opposite the tea merchant Charles Taylor's Café Imperial on Parliament Street. Three further Bettys Tea Rooms opened in York, Northallerton and Ilkley in the 1920s and 1930s, and Frederick built his own bakery in Harrogate to supply them. Eventually, in 1962, Taylors was sold to Bettys, and the present firm of Bettys & Taylors was born. But who was Betty? Various theories have been put forward, and the favourite one seems to be that the tea rooms were named after Betty Lupton, 'the Queen of the Spa' and manager of the Royal Pump Rooms in the 19th century (and see page 31).

FRANCIS FRITH

PIONEER VICTORIAN PHOTOGRAPHER

Francis Frith, founder of the world-famous photographic archive, was a complex and multi-talented man. A devout Quaker and a highly successful Victorian businessman, he was philosophical by nature and pioneering in outlook. By 1855 he had already established a wholesale grocery business in Liverpool, and sold it for the astonishing sum of £200,000, which is the equivalent today of over £15,000,000. Now in his thirties, and captivated by the new science of photography, Frith set out on a series of pioneering journeys up the Nile and to the Near East.

INTRIGUE AND EXPLORATION

He was the first photographer to venture beyond the sixth cataract of the Nile. Africa was still the mysterious 'Dark Continent', and Stanley and Livingstone's historic meeting was a decade into the future. The conditions for picture taking confound belief. He laboured for hours in his wicker dark-room in the sweltering heat of the desert, while the volatile chemicals fizzed dangerously in their trays. Back in London he exhibited his photographs and was 'rapturously cheered' by members of the Royal Society. His reputation as a photographer was made overnight.

VENTURE OF A LIFE-TIME

By the 1870s the railways had threaded their way across the country, and Bank Holidays and half-day Saturdays had been made obligatory by Act of Parliament. All of a sudden the working man and his family were able to enjoy days out, take holidays, and see a little more of the world.

With typical business acumen, Francis Frith foresaw that these new tourists would enjoy having souvenirs to commemorate their days out. For the next thirty years he travelled the country by train and by pony and trap, producing fine photographs of seaside resorts and beauty spots that were keenly bought by millions of Victorians. These prints were painstakingly pasted into family albums and pored over during the dark nights of winter, rekindling precious memories of summer excursions. Frith's studio was soon supplying retail shops all over the country, and by 1890 F Frith & Co had become the greatest specialist photographic publishing company in the world, with over 2,000 sales outlets, and pioneered the picture postcard.

FRANCIS FRITH'S LEGACY

Francis Frith had died in 1898 at his villa in Cannes, his great project still growing. By 1970 the archive he created contained over a third of a million pictures showing 7,000 British towns and villages.

Frith's legacy to us today is of immense significance and value, for the magnificent archive of evocative photographs he created provides a unique record of change in the cities, towns and villages throughout Britain over a century and more. Frith and his fellow studio photographers revisited locations many times down the years to update their views, compiling for us an enthralling and colourful pageant of British life and character.

We are fortunate that Frith was dedicated to recording the minutiae of everyday life. For it is this sheer wealth of visual data, the painstaking chronicle of changes in dress, transport, street layouts, buildings, housing and landscape that captivates us so much today, offering us a powerful link with the past and with the lives of our ancestors.

Computers have now made it possible for Frith's many thousands of images to be accessed almost instantly. The archive offers every one of us an opportunity to examine the places where we and our families have lived and worked down the years. Its images, depicting our shared past, are now bringing pleasure and enlightenment to millions around the world a century and more after his death.

For further information visit: www.francisfrith.com

INTERIOR DECORATION

Frith's photographs can be seen framed and as giant wall murals in thousands of pubs, restaurants, hotels, banks, retail stores and other public buildings throughout Britain. These provide interesting and attractive décor, generating strong local interest and acting as a powerful reminder of gentler days in our increasingly busy and frenetic world.

FRITH PRODUCTS

All Frith photographs are available as prints and posters in a variety of different sizes and styles. In the UK we also offer a range of other gift and stationery products illustrated with Frith photographs, although many of these are not available for delivery outside the UK – see our web site for more information on the products available for delivery in your country.

THE INTERNET

Over 100,000 photographs of Britain can be viewed and purchased on the Frith web site. The web site also includes memories and reminiscences contributed by our customers, who have personal knowledge of localities and of the people and properties depicted in Frith photographs. If you wish to learn more about a specific town or village you may find these reminiscences fascinating to browse. Why not add your own comments if you think they would be of interest to others? See **www.francisfrith.com**

PLEASE HELP US BRING FRITH'S PHOTOGRAPHS TO LIFE

Our authors do their best to recount the history of the places they write about. They give insights into how particular towns and villages developed, they describe the architecture of streets and buildings, and they discuss the lives of famous people who lived there. But however knowledgeable our authors are, the story they tell is necessarily incomplete.

Frith's photographs are so much more than plain historical documents. They are living proofs of the flow of human life down the generations. They show real people at real moments in history; and each of those people is the son or daughter of someone, the brother or sister, aunt or uncle, grandfather or grandmother of someone else. All of them lived, worked and played in the streets depicted in Frith's photographs.

We would be grateful if you would give us your insights into the places shown in our photographs: the streets and buildings, the shops, businesses and industries. Post your memories of life in those streets on the Frith website: what it was like growing up there, who ran the local shop and what shopping was like years ago; if your workplace is shown tell us about your working day and what the building is used for now. Read other visitors' memories and reconnect with your shared local history and heritage. With your help more and more Frith photographs can be brought to life, and vital memories preserved for posterity, and for the benefit of historians in the future.

Wherever possible, we will try to include some of your comments in future editions of our books. Moreover, if you spot errors in dates, titles or other facts, please let us know, because our archive records are not always completely accurate—they rely on 140 years of human endeavour and hand-compiled records. You can email us using the contact form on the website.

Thank you!

For further information, trade, or author enquiries
please contact us at the address below:

The Francis Frith Collection, Frith's Barn, Teffont,
Salisbury, Wiltshire, England SP3 5QP.

Tel: +44 (0)1722 716 376 Fax: +44 (0)1722 716 881
e-mail: sales@francisfrith.co.uk **www.francisfrith.com**